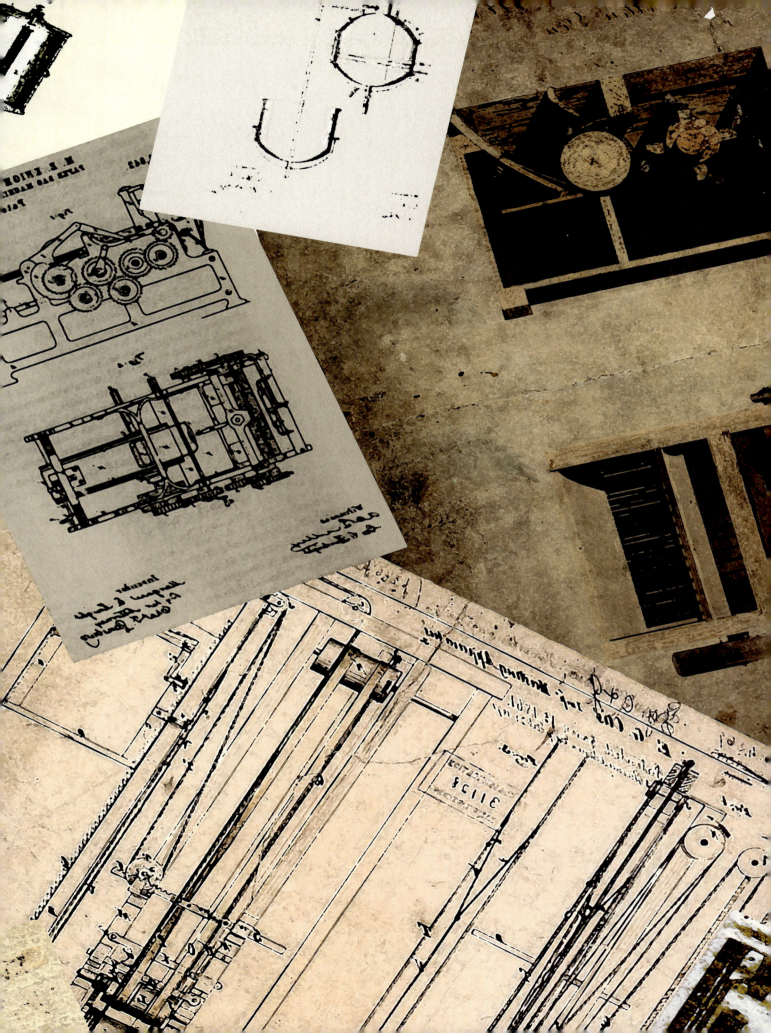

## Picture Credits

t=top, tr=top right, tl=top left, bl= bottom left, br=bottom right, b=bottom, ml=middle left, mr=middle right

Front Cover Images: Joseph-Siffred Duplessis; Joi Ito; Tage Olsin; Older Firearms; Pavel Krok;

Back Cover Images: Steven Bennett

P5: Norman Bruderhofer (b); P6: Tinkeringbell (ml); P6: Tmaurizia (b); P7: Pavel Krok (t); P8: Pearson Scott Foresman (tl); P8: Jonathunder (bl); P8: William Hamilton Gibson (br); P8: Rideau Hall (br); P:9: George Catlin (tl)(br); P8: Saquan Stimpson (tl); P11: W.G. Jackman (tr); P11: Rembrandt Peale (bl); P12: Detroit Publishing Co. (bl); P13: Andrew J. Russell (tl); P13: Hmaag (ml); P13 Carleton E. Watkins (tr); P16: Indianapolis, IN - Madame CJ Walker Manufacturing Company building (ml); P18: George Iles (ml); P18: Brian Cantoni (mr); P20: Jonathunder (tr); P20: HammondCast (br); P21: Zaphod (tl); P21: Håkan Svensson (ml); P21: John Kratz (mr); P21: Rico Shen (br); P23: Rasevic (tr); P25: Dinneen (ml); P26: Mu (ml); P27: Minesweeper (t); P27: Bruce Marlin (tr); P27: Alex Yosifov (mr); P27: Kevin Lawver (br); P28: Pbroks13 (tr); P28: Carrier licensed material courtesy of Carrier Corporation (ml); P29: Magnus Manske (ml); P29: aleehk82 9 (mr); P32: Tage Olsin (tl); P32: soldiersmediacenter (bl); P33: H2okiep (tr); P33: Flying Cloud (tr); P33: soldiersmediacenter (ml); P33: New Brunswick Tourism (br); P33: Alain Carpentier (br); P33: Vincent Baas (br); P34: takomabibelot (tr); P34: Edward Harrison May (tr); P34: M62 (br); P35: M62 (bl); P36: Joseph Barillari (tl); P36: Sybren van Wayenburg (mr); P36: Texas Instruments/wikipedia.org (bl),(bl); P37: Matt Yohe (tr); P37: Apple Inc. (tr); P37: World Economic Forum (ml); P37: Joi (br); P38: Cbro10 (bl),(bl); P36: Håkan Henriksson (mr); P40: Dave Parker (ml); P40: Tammra (mr); P42: Alexander Z. (tl); P42: Charles Willson Peale (tl).

Series Editor:
Sean Kennelly

Fact Check:
Thomas W. Gilman

Written by
Sean Kennelly

Design by
Jonas Fearon Bell

Copyright © 2014 Flowerpot Press,
a Division of Kamalu LLC, Franklin, TN, U.S.A.
and Flowerpot Children's Press, Inc., Oakville, ON, Canada.

All rights reserved. No part of this publication may be reproduced,
stored in a retrieval system or transmitted, in any form or by any means,
electronic, mechanical, photocopying, recording, optical scan, or otherwise, without
the prior written permission of the copyright holder.

Made in China/Fabriqué en Chine

# CONTENTS

| | |
|---|---|
| The Innovative American | 6 |
| Early American Inventions: Native American Innovators | 8 |
| Innovative Colonists | 10 |
| Inventions that Shaped the Nation | 12 |
| Mothers of Invention: Female Innovators | 14 |
| An Innovative Heritage: African-American Inventors | 16 |
| Innovation on the Move | 18 |
| Sending a Message | 20 |
| Industrial Revolutionaries | 22 |
| Healthy Advances | 24 |
| Cooking Up Progress | 26 |
| The Innovation of Comfort | 28 |
| Above and Beyond | 30 |
| A Sporting Chance | 32 |
| Wearing It Well: Clothing Innovations | 34 |
| Digital Visionaries | 36 |
| Playtime! | 38 |
| Entertaining Ideas | 40 |
| Young Innovators | 42 |
| Glossary | 44 |
| Index | 45 |

*Looking for cool and interesting stuff? Watch for WOW facts on the pages of every World of Wonder book!*

# THE INNOVATIVE AMERICAN

Americans have always been a group of creative problem solvers, whether they walked a quiet forest path or the information superhighway.

## INNOVATION

What is innovation? Innovation is all about trying something new. It can be a new invention, or it can just be a new way of doing things. Since the very beginning, America has been one of the most innovative places around. Often called the "melting pot" of the world, people have come to America from distant lands, and together, they have created some pretty useful stuff.

> ### "NECESSITY, THE MOTHER OF INVENTION."
> #### PLATO (427-347 B.C.)
> WHEN SOMEONE NEEDS SOMETHING IT IS CALLED A NECESSITY, AND WHEN WE NEED SOMETHING BADLY ENOUGH WE INVENT NEW THINGS (INVENTIONS) OR NEW WAYS OF DOING THINGS (INNOVATIONS). FROM THE STONE AGE TO THE DIGITAL AGE, MANKIND HAS BEEN SEARCHING FOR WAYS TO IMPROVE THE WORLD AROUND HIM.

## DREAMS INTO ACTION

The only limit to innovation is your imagination. Some people call it "blue sky" thinking when you dream up new ideas. And if you can dream it and you're willing to work hard enough, almost anything is possible! So read on, dream on, and maybe one day you will become a famous inventor like the men, women, and kids in this book!

### IT'S TRUE!

#### - Sticking to It! -

Spencer Silver worked on inventing a super-strong glue. Unfortunately, it was super weak (in other words, NOT very sticky). But a co-worker, Arthur Fry, took the weak glue and put it on the back of paper, creating a multi-million dollar invention called Post-it notes. That's what you call stick-to-it-ivity!

**HELLO!**

## INVENTORS AND INNOVATORS

Inventors and Innovators come in all shapes, sizes, ages, colors, and backgrounds. Sometimes they create things to make work easier, faster, or just plain fun — like when Arthur Gildersleeve wanted to encourage kids to drink more healthy stuff like milk and juice. He bent a straw to make it fun, inventing the Crazy Straw in 1936!

### Famous Firsts

**- One Rock-in' Creation! -**

One day Gary Dahl jokingly complained to his friends how messy pets were and how his pet rock never made a mess. His friends thought it was so funny that he decided to write "The Pet Rock Training Manual" and sold it with a rock. Within months, he was selling over 6,000 Pet Rocks a day, for a total of 1.5 million.

Cool!!

# Early American Inventions:
## Native American Innovators

### Kayak
The kayak was invented by the Inuit Peoples (sometimes called Eskimos) in the Arctic regions of North America. Kayaks (which means "hunter's boat") were made of animal skins stretched over wooden frames. They made it possible for people to travel across icy waters to hunt seal, walrus, and fish. Today, kayaks are used for a variety of purposes, but mostly for recreation.

### It's True!
- Z Force -
While kayaks are used mostly for fun today, during World War II, a group of Australian and English Special Forces soldiers (named Z Force) paddled their kayaks in secret missions to destroy Japanese ships in Singapore!

### Snowshoes
Though primitive shoes for traveling in the snow have been found in Asia, the snowshoes used by most people today were created by the original American inventors—the Eastern First Peoples. Made of bent twigs with leather laces, snowshoes grew out of a need to travel across the deep snows of winter to hunt and gather food.

### Toboggan
Toboggan comes from the Algonquian word "odabaggan." It was also invented by the Eastern First Peoples to help carry food and supplies over the snow. Known as "the hunter's sleigh," toboggans were made from strips of wood or whalebone bound together, with a long, flat bottom and a curved front end. Today, toboggans are used mostly for thrilling rides down snowy slopes.

# Lacrosse

Lacrosse can truly be called the first American sport (sorry, baseball came much later). It was created by Indian tribes in New York and Ontario (Canada). Different villages or tribes would play against each other. They passed a three-inch ball to their teammates with special sticks until they shot the ball into a small goal. The Mohawks called it "the little brother of war," because it was a great way to practice battle skills. And the playing field was huge! The goals could be a few hundred yards to miles apart with no out-of-bounds! Sometimes they played from sunrise to sunset. Whew! What a tough game!

### It's True!

**- You Call it Lacrosse, We Call it... -**
Choctaw – "stick ball"
Eastern Cherokee – "little war"
Mohawk – "little brother of war"
Onondaga – "men hit a rounded object"
Ojibwa – "bump hips"

### - "Give Me a Pair of Bear Paws!" -
Just like modern shoe styles, different snowshoes were introduced by tribes trying to fulfill their needs.

*Alaskan* – Created by Inuit peoples (Eskimos), Alaskan snowshoes are around five feet long. They have upturned noses, similar to modern snow skis, which allow them to slide easily. They were often used to break trails for sled dog teams.

*Michigan* – These snowshoes looked like long tennis racquets. The shoes were very affective for carrying heavy loads of deer, elk, or buffalo since they allowed the weight to be spread out over a large area. Unfortunately, the long tails often got caught on things and made turning around very difficult.

*Ojibwa* – Created by tribes near Manitoba (Canada), these shoes had pointed noses and tails. They were much shorter and wider than the Alaskan or Michigan, allowing the wearer to travel over all kinds of terrain. They even allowed the wearer to walk backwards with ease...well, as easy as it can be in deep snow.

*Bear Paw* – Oval-shaped, these shoes were made mainly for quick and easy travel over the snowy hills.

# INNOVATIVE COLONISTS

While the bells of liberty were ringing throughout the land, a revolution of innovation was just beginning.

## BENJAMIN FRANKLIN

While Franklin was responsible for helping form a new type of government, he spent much of his life coming up with new inventions that we still use today. In his day, Franklin saw many buildings damaged by lightning, so he came up with a metal rod or "lightning rod" (1749) to channel the raw electricity safely to the ground. (Of course, he was also famous for flying a kite in a storm to prove his theories about electricity.)

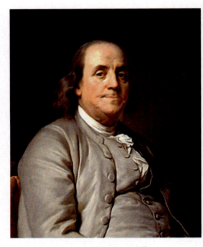

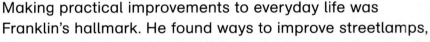

 IT'S TRUE!

- Glad to Share -
Benjamin Franklin never patented any of his inventions. His philosophy? "As we benefit from the inventions of others, we should be glad to share our own...freely and gladly."

He also found that he could combine his normal eyeglasses with his reading glasses. He did this by cutting both lenses in half and blending the two halves into a single frame—thus creating bifocals (1760s), a style of eyeglasses still in use today!

Making practical improvements to everyday life was Franklin's hallmark. He found ways to improve streetlamps, musical instruments (inventing the glass harmonica in 1761), and the postal system (he was the first postmaster). He also created a wood stove that provided more heat with less wood (the Franklin stove in 1742). He even constructed a foot-operated fan for his reading chair!

You could also call him one of the original American conservationists. He once wrote a witty letter about an "economical project" to save energy and reduce the need to burn as many candles or oil lamps. His idea was very similar to something we call Daylight Savings Time today. As Ben said in his famous book, *Poor Richard's Almanac*, "A penny saved is a penny earned." No wonder we find this thrifty inventor on the face of the $100 bill!

## ELI WHITNEY

The "father of American technology," Whitney came up with a machine to separate the fibers and seeds of the cotton plant—the cotton gin (his landmark invention created in 1793). It made processing cotton much easier and led to a boom in the cotton industry that made America a major cotton supplier to the world.

Yet Whitney had other ideas, such as the first mass-produced interchangeable gun parts. His method soon started the American factory system and opened the door to the Industrial Revolution.

# OLIVER EVANS

An ambitious young man, Evans apprenticed himself to a wheelwright (someone who made wagon and carriage wheels) at 16 years old. Later, he created an invention that many colonists used, including George Washington—the first automated flour mill (1787).

Evans even came up with a design for a refrigeration machine in 1805 (though he never actually built the machine—another inventor did that 30 years later). His greatest contribution to America may have been the invention of the high-pressure steam engine. This innovation would be used to power a variety of vehicles including Evans' own steam carriage, the *Orukter Amphibolos*—the first true horseless carriage or automobile.

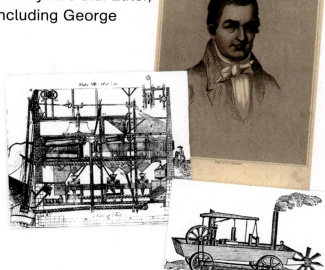

# THOMAS JEFFERSON

Jefferson was not only America's 3rd President (whose face can be found on the U.S. $2 bill and the nickel), but he was a busy inventor as well. The swivel chairs we use today got their start when Jefferson created a new kind of chair with a seat that could spin around. Then, he put the chair to use as he wrote the Declaration of Independence.

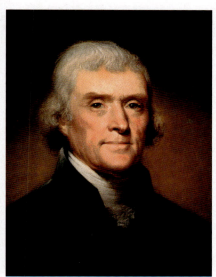

And though he shared Ben Franklin's ideas about sharing inventions, he felt protecting inventions would actually encourage creative minds to make more helpful devices and systems. So he helped pass the first U.S. patent law in 1790. The law made it illegal to copy someone's invention without their permission

One of Jefferson's more historic inventions was the spy decoder wheel. It was known as the Jefferson disk or "wheel cipher" (1795). The cipher was a series of wooden disks on a spindle that allowed the user to code and decode secret messages. His invention was so helpful that it was even used in World War II!

11

# Inventions that Shaped the Nation

As America grew and expanded over a vast continent, inventions were needed. These inventions spanned the miles of rugged frontier bringing needed information, supplies and order to the wild new territory.

## Commercial Steamboats

Though Robert Fulton did not invent the steamboat (William Henry created the first one in 1763, which promptly sunk), he is often called the "father of steam navigation." Strangely, he started out as an artist and even exhibited some of his work in London at the Royal Gallery. Then, he decided to turn his efforts to more practical works such as designing submarines called "diving boats" for both the French and the British Navy. He even

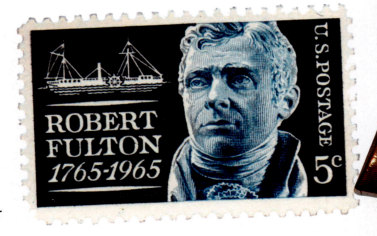

designed the first practical submarine, the *Nautilus*, for Napoleon Bonaparte. He also designed some of the first "torpedoes" and successfully blew up a 300-ton ship in a field test. The idea of building a steamboat was always on his mind.

**It's True!**

- A Painter? -

Fulton got his start as a portrait painter, painting famous people including fellow inventor Benjamin Franklin.

After months of building models and changing the design, Fulton finally built his ship. It was called *The North River Steamboat* (later named *The Clermont*). It had dual-paddle wheels, luxury sleeping compartments, and a saloon. Though many people made fun of his flat-bottomed boat design, labeling it "Fulton's folly," the inventor had the last laugh when his ship became a successful business running up and down the Hudson River. Before long, many steam ships moved people and supplies on nearly every river in America.

# Transcontinental Railroad

Like most innovators, Theodore Judah had a dream: to build a railroad across America to California. When people heard his idea, they began to call him "Crazy Judah." Still, he believed trains that could cross the mountains and prairies would allow people to travel west safely and would make a lot of money. Though many people turned him down, Judah convinced four businessmen in Sacramento to invest in his idea for a railroad over the Sierra Nevada Mountains. Of course, that was just the beginning. Later, he convinced the U.S. government to pass the 1862 Pacific Railroad Act, which made the construction of the first transcontinental railroad possible. However, six years before the railroad was completed, Judah traveled by ship to New York and caught yellow fever in Panama along the way. He died before the railroad was finished—a trip that future travelers would take by train, thanks to Mr. Judah.

# Colt Revolver

As a young boy of 11, Samuel Colt read of the "impossible" tasks of Robert Fulton and others. When he heard soldiers talk about how hard it would be to create a gun that would shoot five or six times, Colt decided to be an inventor. He set out to make the "impossible" gun the soldiers described. Though he wasn't the first to create a revolver, Colt's pistol was the weapon that "won the West." It allowed settlers and lawmen alike to fire multiple shots without reloading, which often made the difference between life and death. Colt was also the first to mass-produce thousands of guns using an assembly line process.

# Telegraph & Morse Code

Samuel Morse never set out to be an inventor, but an artist. After schooling in London, he was commissioned to paint portraits of famous people such as President James Monroe, inventor Eli Whitney, dictionary maker Noah Webster, and the Marquis de Lafayette. Later, he even tried his hand at early photography, training the future Civil War photographer Matthew Brady. But during a trip home from Europe, Morse heard about experiments with electricity, and his creative mind began to spin. The result? The single wire telegraph that used electrical pulses to send messages. The new invention used Morse's own code (Morse code) for each letter of the alphabet. The first message, "What hath God wrought?" was sent in 1844 from Washington D.C. to Baltimore, MD, and soon telegraph lines connected the country and the world.

# Mothers of Invention: Female Innovators

Men weren't the only ones to come up with some innovative ideas. The contribution of female inventors has a long history in America. In fact, in 1809 Mary Kies created a unique process to weave silk and thread into straw hats. She was the first woman to be awarded a patent for her new idea. And she wouldn't be the last.

## Margaret Knight

Known as the "Female Edison," Knight patented her first invention at the age of 30. She went on to patent nearly 90 inventions, including textile and shoe-making machines. In 1871, she invented the first square-bottomed paper bag machine (until then, paper bags were more like envelopes)! Ironically, when workmen were installing her machine at a factory, they refused to listen to her advice. They said, "What does a woman know about machines?" If only they knew.

## Stephanie Kwolek

With a bachelor's degree in chemistry, Kwolek (working for chemical giant DuPont) came up with a new fiber called "Kevlar." Woven like tiny spider webs, Kevlar is so strong, it can stop bullets. It is used as body armor for the military and police. It is also used in everything from bike frames to tornado shelters!

### It's True!

**- A Woman's Touch -**
Catherine Greene, wife of Revolutionary War General Nathanael Greene, gave the idea for the cotton gin to a mechanical handyman who rented a room from her. His name? Eli Whitney.

14

# Grace Hopper

Known by many as "Amazing Grace," Hopper believed computer programming could be written in English. She came up with the computer source language, FLOW-MATIC, which she later helped develop into COBOL (which stands for Common Business Oriented Language) while she worked for the U.S. Navy. She was also the third person (and first woman) to program the Harvard Mark I computer (also called the IBM ASCC), one of the first computers in 1944.

In later years, Hopper attained the rank of Rear Admiral. In 1969, she was awarded the first ever Computer Science Man-of-the-Year Award from the Data Processing Management Association. And in 1973, she became the first person from the United States (and the first woman) to be made a Distinguished Fellow of the British Computer Society. Amazing!

## Famous Firsts

### - A Vision-ary Woman -
Patricia Bath was the first female African-American doctor to get a patent for a medical purpose. Her device? The Cataract Laserphaco Probe. Her invention helped people with cataracts regain their vision. (Cataracts are a cloudy area on the lens of the eye which makes it hard to see clearly.)

## Rose Totino

Born the daughter of Italian immigrants, Rose Totino knew that hard work was the key to success. So, when a banker wouldn't give her and her husband a loan to start their pizza business, she baked a fresh pizza and brought it to the banker. He was convinced! Soon Totino's Italian Kitchen opened in Minneapolis, MN, offering take-out pizza. But her dream was to offer frozen pizzas that people could take home and cook anytime. So she experimented for years, and in 1979, finally came up with a pizza dough for frozen pizzas that didn't taste like the "cardboard" dough of other companies. Today, as a result of her hard work, Totino's is one of the best-selling frozen pizzas on the market!

# An Innovative Heritage:
## African American Inventors

Until the abolition of slavery, only free black inventors were allowed to patent their creations. Many did not since being famous could also stir up prejudice. Still, African-American inventors bravely continued to dream and filled America with innovative ideas.

## Sarah Breedlove McWilliams Walker
### a.k.a. Madam C.J. Walker

Sarah Breedlove McWilliams Walker, better known as Madame Walker, was the daughter of former slaves. Her parents died when she was seven, and her husband died when she was 20. She then left her native Louisiana and went to St. Louis, Missouri, where she began selling her homemade beauty products (make-up, hair creams, etc.) door-to-door. People liked her products so much, she had to keep hiring more and more people to sell them. Soon there were over 3,000 people working for her. She became the first African-American business woman to become a self-made millionaire. As she got older, she retired among the wealthy in a spacious home on the Hudson River next to business tycoon John D. Rockefeller.

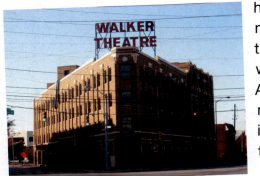

## Granville T. Woods

Known as the "Black Edison," Granville Woods created a number of inventions to improve electric railway cars. He even invented a system for letting a railroad engineer know how close his train was to other trains. Alexander Graham Bell's company bought one of his inventions, and Thomas Edison offered Woods a job, but he declined. He liked inventing and working for himself.

## Garrett Morgan

After trying to rescue some men trapped in a smoky Cleveland, Ohio, tunnel under Lake Erie, Garrett Morgan invented a gas inhaler to help rescuers breathe while in smoke-filled places. Though racial prejudice made it tough for him to sell his invention, the U.S. Army used the inhaler as gas masks for soldiers in World War I. Firefighters today use a similar breathing device to help them safely enter burning buildings.

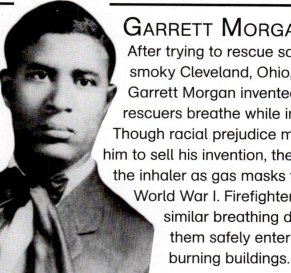

## George Washington Carver

George Washington Carver was definitely an uncommon man. Born the son of slaves, he rose up to become one of the great agricultural innovators of the South. He took a crop, the peanut, that was once only used to feed pigs, and found 325 uses for it. He also found 118 uses for sweet potatoes. Strangely, he only patented three of his discoveries. His reason? "God gave them to me," he said, "How can I sell them to someone else?"

### - George Washington Carver -
*"When you can do the common things in life in an uncommon way, you will command the attention of the world."*

## It's True!

### - The Real McCoy -

Elijah McCoy earned more than 50 patents, but the most famous one was the McCoy lubricator. It was a cup that poured oil through a small tube to help machine ball bearings roll smoothly. Others tried to copy his invention, but everyone wanted the real thing or "the real McCoy!"

# Innovation on the Move

Transportation was key to the early expansion of the United States. By land, river, sea, and air, Americans pressed on across North America and beyond. It took many creative minds to find new ways to get from here to there!

## Steaming Away

Creator of the steamboat, John Fitch saw a drawing of an early British steam engine in an encyclopedia, but Britain would not allow the export of new technology to its former colony. However, Fitch attempted to design his own version of a steam engine and got clockmaker and inventor Henry Voigt to help him build a working model and place it on a boat.

The first successful trial run of his steamboat, *Perseverance*, was made on the Delaware River on August 22, 1787. Many delegates from the Constitutional Convention were there, and he hoped to raise money to pay for his ship. Instead, he got lots of compliments on his creation—the first steamboat!

## Burn Rubber

Charles Goodyear decided to become an inventor at age 33. He suffered through a series of financial problems and failures (some of which landed him in jail) before discovering a way to process the sap of the rubber tree. He turned it into a compound that would not melt when it got hot, a process called "vulcanizing" (1839). Unfortunately, Goodyear never got to profit from his invention. After his death in 1860, his son sold the rights to the Goodyear name. Later, the Goodyear Tire and Rubber Company was created.

## THE SKY'S THE LIMIT

The Wright brothers, Orville and Wilbur, were two Americans credited with inventing and building the world's first successful airplane. They used mechanical skills they gained working on bicycles, motors, and other machinery. They also studied the work of other inventors such as Leonardo da Vinci and Sir George Cayley, and came to believe that a true flying machine could be controlled and balanced with practice.

After a number of crashes and mishaps, the Wrights finally created a three-axis control. This control allowed the pilot to safely steer their flying machine. Armed with their new controls, the brothers traveled from their Ohio workshop to the Outer Banks of North Carolina. Then, on December 17, 1903, Orville Wright piloted the Wright Flyer over the sand dunes of Kitty Hawk, NC, and right into the pages of history!

## LONG DISTANCE TRIPPE

An original blue sky dreamer, young Juan Trippe became a pilot for the U.S. Navy during World War I. When the war ended before he saw action, he turned his efforts to creating a passenger airplane service that eventually became Pan American Airways (or Pan Am as it was later known). Yet, his greatest innovation had to be his development of the first long-range passenger plane (3,000 miles or more) known as the Clipper flying boat. With it, Pan Am became the first airline to cross the Pacific! Each Clipper carried over 70 passengers to such far off places as Hawaii and Asia. It even had private dressing rooms and a dining area serving gourmet food! No wonder Indiana Jones flew on a Clipper in so many of his movie travels!

### IT'S TRUE!

- The Wright Way -

The Wright brothers didn't drink or smoke and refused to fly on Sundays. For safety, and as a promise to their father, Wilbur and Orville did not fly together. But Orville did fly their father once as he exclaimed with delight, "Higher, Orville, higher!"

# Sending a Message

Americans love to communicate! From writing letters to sending video and text messages on our cell phones, we have a driving need to be heard. So, it comes as no surprise that inventors from around the country have come up with some cool inventions that changed the way we speak to each other.

### Alexander Graham Bell
Telephone (1876)
On March 10, 1876, three days after beating inventor Elisha Gray to the patent office, Alexander Graham Bell spoke his famous words, "Mr. Watson, come here! I want to see you!" Mr. Watson, Bell's assistant, heard the words through Bell's new invention, the telephone, and came running from another room. Before long, the first telephone networks sprang up around the country. Ironically, Bell refused to have a telephone in his study. He considered his most famous invention an intrusion on his real work as a scientist.

### Edwin Howard Armstrong
Wide-Band FM radio (1933)
Born in New York City, Edwin Howard Armstrong always had a fascination with radio. He even built his own 125-foot radio tower in his backyard in Yonkers. Years later, he studied and then taught at Columbia University where he created wide-band FM, or frequency modulation. He also invented the radio tuner that allows radios to change channels and frequencies. Though superior to AM radio in sound quality, FM would not gain wide acceptance until after his death in 1954. You could say FM was the "wave" of the future!

## Philo Farnsworth
### Television (1927)

Like many inventors, Philo Farnsworth created many inventions. His most famous one was the world's first all-electronic television in 1927. The technology he created to scan and receive the images was inspired by his days as an Idaho farm boy when he used a back-and-forth motion to plow a field. The result was literally something to "see," though it would be years before television became as common as radio.

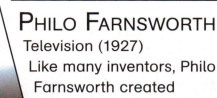

## George Eastman
### Snapshot Camera (1888)

They say a picture is worth a thousand words, so inventor George Eastman took that to heart and created a camera that everyone could afford. The Kodak "snapshot" camera (1888) allowed the average person to take their own pictures rather than go to an expensive photographer. He even created the transparent film used in the cameras (1885). That film also paved the way for flexible film rolls that Thomas Edison would use with his new invention—the motion picture camera.

## Famous Firsts

### - Can You Hear Me Now? -

Martin Cooper invented the first "cell" phone in 1973. They were originally called "mobile" phones, but you'd need a backpack to lug this baby around to classes. And texting was just a glimmer in some inventor's eye.

# Industrial Revolutionaries

Inventions triggered the Industrial Revolution. New ideas thrived, making life easier and factories more productive. Innovation was here to stay!

## Thomas Edison

From his childhood, Thomas Alva Edison loved to experiment. He was captivated by the natural forces of fire and electricity. Not surprisingly, he got his first of over 1,000 U.S. patents at the ripe old age of 22. Of all American inventors, Edison stands out for the number of innovations he brought to the world. Some of his most famous inventions were the phonograph (1877), an old-fashioned way of listening to music or other sounds, his motion picture camera named the Kinetograph in 1891, and, of course, the electric light bulb in 1879. People were so amazed by his inventions that they called him "The Wizard of Menlo Park," since his laboratory was located in Menlo Park, New Jersey (now Edison, NJ). Innovation was practically his middle name!

## Cyrus McCormick

Cyrus McCormick worked on his family farm from an early age. He followed in the footsteps of his father, Robert McCormick, and constantly came up with inventions to make their farm work easier. His greatest invention was something his father started—a mechanical reaper or harvester (1834). Before the mechanical reaper, workers had to hand cut wheat and other grains and bundle them—something that took a lot of work and time. McCormick's invention changed the way farming was done. It made farms more productive, so they needed fewer workers. Therefore, the workers found city jobs that sped up the industrial revolution in America. Soon, the United States was the king of industrial nations.

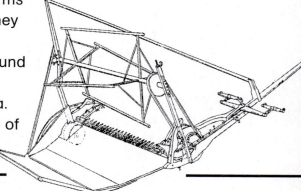

# Nikola Tesla

One of the more mysterious and unsung American innovators is Nikola Tesla. A first-class dreamer even as a boy, Tesla created an engine powered by insects that he glued to a paper wheel. He could also visualize inventions in his mind, complete with every detail. He could see it so

clearly that he built his inventions without a blueprint. His inventions rivaled that of Edison, his main competitor! What were some of them? If you ever played with a remote control toy, thank Tesla. He invented the radio remote control (1898). He also came up with the ideas behind the AC (alternating current) power you use to charge your toys at home. He also created an "electric igniter" or spark plug for gas engines as early as 1898. What a visionary inventor!

## It's True!

- Tuning in Tesla -

According to a 1943 U.S. Supreme Court ruling just a few years after his death, Nikola Telsa was the true inventor of the radio, not Guglielmo Marconi.

# Henry Ford

The horseless carriage (we call them cars or automobiles) was not invented by Henry Ford. He didn't invent the auto assembly line (Eli Olds did that in 1901). What did he do? He was the first one to lower the cost so that "every man" could buy a car. How'd he do it? The first conveyor-belt based assembly line. With it, he was able to cut assembly time from 12 hours to just 93 minutes to make his famous Model-T Ford! By 1927, Ford Motor Company had made over 15 million Model-Ts, making it the biggest manufacturer of automobiles in the world.

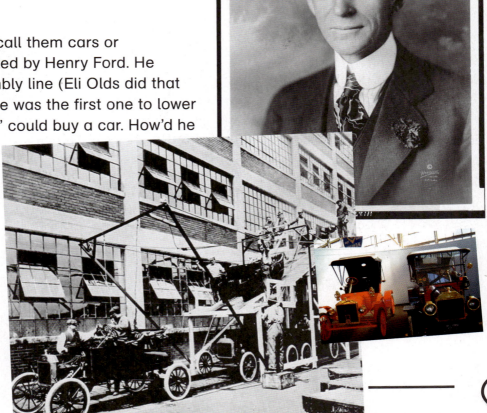

23

# Healthy Advances

Since the founding of the United States, health technology has come a long way, saving lives and easing the discomforts of everyday Americans.

## Adhesive Bandages (1921)

Josephine Dickson was always cutting or burning her fingers in the kitchen while preparing food. She would often bandage her wounds with cotton gauze and adhesive tape, but the bandage would often fall off her very active fingers. Worried about her safety, Josephine's husband, Earle Dickson (who worked as a cotton buyer for the Johnson & Johnson Company), decided to create a better bandage. He put a small square of gauze on a piece of adhesive tape and covered it with a piece of crinoline (a stiff material) to keep the wound free of dirt and germs. His company, Johnson & Johnson, loved the idea! Soon Band-Aids were a household name, and Dickson was made a company vice-president!

## Polio Vaccine (1955)

Much more serious than a cut or burn, polio was once considered the most frightening public health problem of the post-war United States. In fact, during the epidemic of 1952, there were nearly 58,000 cases reported. Of those, 3,145 people died from the disease and 21,269 had some form of paralysis—most of them kids. The disease spared no one. Even President Franklin D. Roosevelt was stricken with polio in 1921. Roosevelt led the way, and scientists were in a frantic race to find a cure. Enter Jonas Salk who, in 1948, devoted himself to finding a solution. Seven years later, in 1955, Salk and his research team developed a successful vaccine! He was soon hailed as a "miracle worker" by the nation. Yet, like many inventors before him, Salk had no interest in making money from his creation. When asked in a TV interview about who owned the patent to the new vaccine, Salk simply told them, "There is no patent. Could you patent the Sun?"

Salk's work continued for years afterwards. He founded the Salk Institute for Biological Studies in La Jolla, California, which is today a center for medical and scientific research. A medical pioneer to the end, Salk spent the last years of his life searching for a vaccine against HIV.

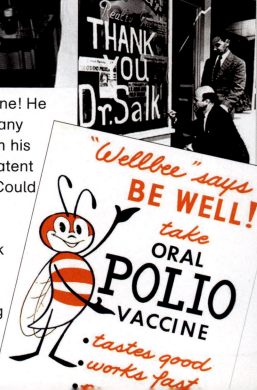

## Blood Bank (1937)

Charles Drew discovered that if he separated the liquid red blood cells from the near solid plasma and froze them separately, blood could be saved in a "blood bank" until it was needed. His work saved the lives of many wounded soldiers in World War II. After the war, he became the first director of the American Red Cross Blood Bank.

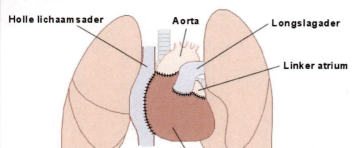

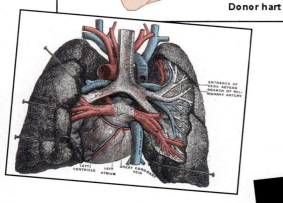

### Famous Firsts

- Transplants R Us! -
American doctors were the first to successfully transplant bone marrow (1956), and lungs (1963)!

## Deodorant (1941)

What a breath of fresh creative air! In olden-times, people used lots of perfume or cologne to cover up icky body smells. Thanks to Jules Montenier, people started smelling better by using his invention, deodorant. They also sweat less due to anti-perspirant, another creation he devised, which is still in use today.

# Cooking Up Progress

The kitchen is one of the most creative environments on Earth. Many American inventors have been hard at work for years creating new foods and treats that have delighted generations.

## Condensed Milk (1856)

Gail Borden tried for years to get his idea off the ground. He invented condensed milk – milk where the water is taken out and sugar is added. When it is canned, it lasts for several years until it's opened. Years later, during the American Civil War, the Union Army used his creation to feed their soldiers – one of the early steps that propelled his compay, Borden, to great success today. Condensed milk is still used in sweet treats from cookies to pumpkin pie!

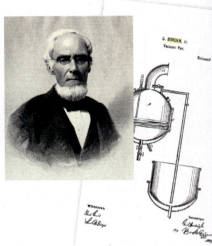

### It's True

- Chinese Fortune Cookies (1914) -
The famous "Chinese" treat is not from China, but rather Japanese-Americans living in California. They based the treat on Japanese crackers with "fortune slips" which are sold in temples and shrines in Japan.

## Flash Frozen Foods (1923)

When he went north to do research on ticks and Rocky Mountain spotted fever, Clarence Birdseye was taught by the Inuit (Eskimos) to ice fish. He found that in -40°F weather, the fish froze almost instantly, but tasted fresh when thawed.

So Birdseye established his own company and created a patented double-belt freezer (1925) to freeze fish and seafood. Eventually, he began using the same process to freeze all kinds of fruits, vegetables, and other meats. Today, the name "Birds Eye" remains a leading frozen food company. Pretty cool!

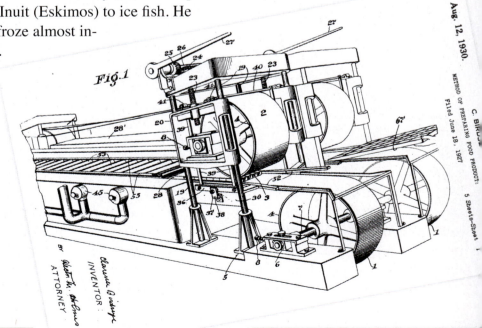

## Fast Food

America has always been a nation on the go! When automobiles were invented, the need for meals that could be purchased and eaten on-demand grew. So American innovators came up with some new ideas. Joseph Horn & Frank Hardart's Automat (1902), a collection of vending machines with an attendant, came first. Then, in 1948, the first drive-thru (In 'N Out) was created. Yet it was milkshake mixer salesman, Ray Kroc, who took the idea of a fast-food restaurant and spread it across the country. He bought the rights to expand the McDonald brothers' fast-food restaurant (something called a franchise – a license to sell a company's products in a certain area). Soon Kroc made McDonald's a household name that still dominates the fast-food scene!

## Sweets & Treats

Americans have had a long love affair with sweets and munchies. Here are just a few of their more original concoctions.

**Doughnuts (1847)** – Tired of undercooked fried dough on-board his ship, Captain Hanson Gregory cut a hole in the middle of the dough, and doughnuts were born!

**Potato Chips (1853)** – Wanting to teach a complaining patron a lesson, chef George Crum sliced up an order of French-fried potatoes almost paper thin. Then he fried them until they were crunchy and splashed, them with lots of salt. The patron loved them! And so did everyone ever since!

**Cotton Candy (1897)** – William Morrison & John C. Wharton, a team from Nashville, Tennessee, created an electric machine that spun sugar in the silky threads which they originally called "fairy floss." They introduced the sweet treat at the 1904 World's Fair in St. Louis, Missouri.

**Bubble Gum (1928)** – Accountant Walter Diemer loved to play around with gum recipes in his spare time. One time he accidentally created a gum that stretched more easily but was less sticky than regular gum. He called it bubble gum, since you could blow bubbles with it. Originally, he wanted to color his new gum blue (his favorite color), but the only dye at the factory was pink. So most bubble gum today is…pink!

**Chocolate Chip Cookies (1930)** – One day Ruth Wakefield cut up bits of a Nestle semi-sweet chocolate bar (quite literally "chips") to add to her cookies for her guests at the Toll House Inn. At the time, she had no idea what she had started. Nestle loved her recipe so much that they gave her a lifetime supply of chocolate. She just had to let them print her recipe on the wrapper of each chocolate bar and later…bags of chocolate chips!

# The Innovation of Comfort

Making life easier and more comfortable has often been the aim of many inventors. Americans love innovation and greet each new creation with a sigh of relief and a smile of blissful satisfaction!

## Air Conditioning (1906)

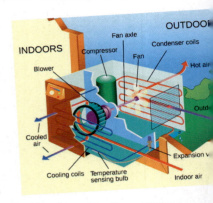

A New York printing company found the humidity and heat in its factory were causing problems with their printing. So they called on a recent Cornell University engineering graduate, 25-year-old Willis Carrier. On July 17, 1902, Carrier submitted drawings for the world's first modern air conditioning system. A few years later, in 1906, Carrier was granted a patent on his cool new invention. By the 1920s, air conditioning became available in homes across the United States. Soon, thousands of Americans were flocking to the "Sun Belt," the dry southwest and humid southeastern areas of the country that were once considered hard to live in because it was so hot. Carrier definitely became the nationwide king of cool. Even today, the Carrier name continues to offer relief from the scorching summer heat!

## Modern Elevator (1852)

Though he wasn't the first one to create some kind of elevator (even the ancient Romans had elevators), Elisha Otis was the first one to create an elevator that could rise to great heights safely. Called the "Safety Elevator" (1852), Otis' design did away with hydraulic elevators that required deep pits to operate. The pits made it impossible to build high buildings. So Otis' innovation actually made the modern skyscrapers of today possible! Similar to our elevators today, Otis' invention featured a braking system. He demonstrated it at the New York Exposition in a dramatic, death-defying presentation in 1854. A few years later, the first Otis passenger elevator made its debut at 488 Broadway Avenue in New York City. Soon, skyscrapers popped up in New York, Chicago, and other cities around the country. Today, the Otis Elevator Company, now a subsidiary of United Technologies Corporation, is the world's largest manufacturer of vertical transport systems.

# Microwave Oven (1945)

Back in 1945, a self-taught engineer named Percy Spencer was building magnetrons—something that creates microwaves—for a radar set. As he worked, he discovered that a chocolate bar in his pocket had melted. So he began to experiment, and finally he perfected the process of heating using microwaves. He encased his new machine in a metal box, and his employer, Raytheon, patented the creation in 1945—the microwave oven. The first commercial microwave oven was a monster machine that weighed 750 pounds (340 kg) and was nearly six feet tall (1.8 m). It was water-cooled and cost around five thousand dollars. What a beast! Thank goodness they figured out how to make them smaller!

# Segway Personal Transporter (2001)

When Dean Kamen created the Segway personal transporter in 2001, it looked like something out of science-fiction movie. The Segway is controlled by computers and powered by electric motors in the base of the machine. It can stay balanced with a rider standing on it, despite the lack of a third wheel. It does this with the help of five gyroscopic self-balancing sensors and two tilt sensors. And though it hasn't caught on everywhere yet, it's hard to deny that the transporter is a clean futuristic engineering marvel!

## It's True!

### - Protecting the Family Name -

Creators of rolled toilet paper (1890), Edward and Clarence Scott founded the Scott Paper Company in 1879. Though it's a name you still see on store shelves today, at first the company did not market their products under the Scott brand name. The reason? They didn't want to, uh…"soil" the family's good name.

# Above and Beyond

While some inventions have lifted us to heights beyond our imagination, not all of them are the work of one individual. Often the work of many innovators come together to create some of the greatest American achievements.

## Liquid Fuel Rocket & Multi-Stage Rocket Designs (1915)

*"Every vision is a joke until the first man accomplishes it; once realized, it becomes commonplace."* – **Robert Goddard**

Practically born with stars in his eyes, Robert Goddard first dreamed of space after reading H.G. Wells' classic science fiction novel, *The War of the Worlds.* At 17, his imagination blossomed as he climbed a cherry tree to cut limbs on his family's rural farm. The view on that October day in 1899 inspired him to create a device he felt "had even the possibility of ascending to Mars."

The boy who came down from the tree was forever fueled by a futuristic vision. Goddard's vision drove him to create over 200 patented inventions that powered the early space program of the United States. The work he did laid the foundations of the *Saturn V* rocket that carried American astronauts into space and beyond. And though his early rockets never got to the Moon, it could be said that this was one inventor whose imagination really blasted off!

### It's True!

**- Anniversary Day -**

Robert Goddard celebrated the day of his greatest inspiration—the day he climbed the cherry tree as a boy on October 19th, 1899—as "Anniversary Day." In his words, he was a "different boy" when he came down from the tree and felt a sense of purpose ever after.

# Nuclear Submarines – *U.S.S. Nautilus* (1955)

Americans have been fascinated with the depths of liquid space from the early days of the nation. In 1955, the United States launched the world's first nuclear-powered submarine, the U.S.S. *Nautilus*. It was the fourth ship to be named after the famous sub in Jules Verne's *Twenty Thousand Leagues Under the Sea*. Unlike other subs, the *Nautilus* never needed refueling, and it could operate at high speeds for long periods of time. Best of all, it could stay underwater for up to four months! It even went under the North Pole in 1958!

## Space Shuttle (1981)

Though development of the Space Shuttle began in 1969, it wasn't until 1981 that the dream became a reality. On April 12th, 1981, Space Shuttle *Columbia* lifted off at Cape Canaveral, Florida, and became the world's first reusable spacecraft. Designed by a team of scientists and engineers, the shuttle fleet included five functional orbiters: *Columbia, Challenger, Discovery, Atlantis,* and *Endeavour*. (The first shuttle, *Enterprise*, was only designed for approach and landing tests.)

# Optical Space Telescope (1990)

Though physicist and astronomer Lyman Spitzer had pushed for a space-based optical telescope since 1946, it wasn't until the space shuttle program that such an invention was possible. Named after early American astronomer Edwin Hubble, the Hubble Space Telescope was pushed into orbit by Space Shuttle *Discovery* on April 24th, 1990. After a few repairs, the Hubble sent back stunning pictures of our universe and star systems beyond our galaxy. Pretty spacey stuff!

# A Sporting Chance

Americans have always enjoyed a good physical challenge. They may call it "play," but most sports push, pull, and keep you moving!

## Baseball (1845)

Though not everyone can agree, most historians credit Alexander Cartwright (not Abner Doubleday), with creating the game of baseball. The idea came from a game played locally in New York City near Cartwright's Manhattan bookstore. It was played with a stick and ball, and the kids called it "town ball." Cartwright decided to create a diamond-shaped field, made a set of rules, and the game quickly caught on. Since that time, baseball has truly become America's national pastime.

## American Football (1879)

Football, as it's known in the United States, borrowed ideas from British rugby and similar games. But it was Walter Camp, considered the "Father of American Football," who made new rules. He added a line of scrimmage and down-and-distance rules that shaped it into what we see on the gridiron today.

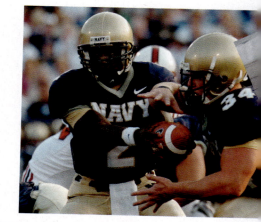

### Famous Firsts

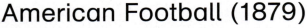

- Basketball: Made in Canada? -

Well, not really. But basketball was invented by a Canadian doctor by the name of James Naismith. He was a teacher at a college in Springfield, Massachusetts, in 1891 when he came up with the game.

## Volleyball (1895)

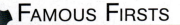

Taking some ideas from tennis and handball, Holyoke, Massachusetts, YMCA director William Morgan created a game he called "Mintonette." It was designed to be played indoors and was supposed to be less "rough" than basketball (a new sport at the time that had been created just ten miles away in Springfield, MA). Thankfully, Alfred Halstead saw the first exhibition match in 1896 and renamed it "volleyball!"

# Water Skiing (1922)

Ralph Samuelson thought skiing could be done on water as well as snow. So the 18-year-old Minnesotan tried to ski on everything from wooden barrel slats to snow skis. Finally, he created his own wooden skis out of two 8-feet by 9-inch boards. He also attached two leather straps to hold his feet in place. Using a long rope fashioned from a window sash with a ring at the end, Samuelson had his brother pull him with their boat. As the boat started up, Samuelson leaned back. Before long, he was riding on top of the water! For the next 15 years, Samuelson traveled all over America, showing people his new sport of water skiing.

# Stock Car Racing (1936)

Stock car racing actually got its start during the age of Prohibition. Bootleg whiskey was often transported by drivers who used modified street cars to avoid being caught by local police. Yet when the law was changed in 1933, many drivers still enjoyed driving fast and started racing for pride and prize money. One of the first big races was held at Daytona Beach, Florida, on March 8, 1936. There, a collection of racers gathered to determine who the fastest cars and drivers were. While only 10 of 27 cars finished the race, a young Bill France placed 5th. France would go on to organize NASCAR—the National Association for Stock Car Racing in 1947. Dreamers, start your engines!

# Snowboarding (1965)

Engineer Sherman Poppen wanted to create a toy for his daughter to ride on the snowy slopes of Muskegon, Michigan. So Poppen fastened two skis together and created the "snurfer" in 1965. Over the next ten years, he sold nearly a million snurfers. Soon snurfing competitions were being held at ski resorts. Skateboarders and surfers came to the competitions looking for a new adrenaline rush. One of those early snurfers was 14-year-old Jake Burton Carpenter. Years later, he founded Burton Snowboards. Talk about catching a wave of innovation!

## It's True!

- The Zamboni (1949) -

The famous ice resurfacer used around the world for hockey and ice skating was actually invented by Californian Frank J. Zamboni.

# Wearing it Well: Clothing Innovations

A stitch in time may save nine, but Americans have created quite a few machines, materials, and miscellaneous accessories!

## Sewing Machine

French tailor Barthélemy Thimonnier was the first to patent and operate a working sewing machine in 1830. Believe it or not, other tailors actually destroyed his machines, fearing they would be out of work. But it was Isaac Singer who refined the machine in 1850. He made it affordable for anyone to buy his machines through installment payments. As a result, sales took off! He also started the first international U.S. company, I.M. Singer & Co., with offices in Paris, France, and Rio de Janeiro, Brazil. Though there were some disputes over who invented the modern sewing machine, Singer managed to do better than any of his competitors. And the Singer Corporation still makes sewing machines today!

### It's True!

**- A Genuine Singer -**
To sell his sewing machines, Isaac Singer would…sing! Willing to go to any length to get people's attention, Singer would entertain crowds with his singing talents. While he sang, a pretty girl would demonstrate the new sewing machine.

## Denim Jeans

In late 1872, Jacob Davis, a Reno, Nevada, tailor, started making men's work pants with metal rivets at the points of strain. He wanted to patent the process but needed a business helper. So he turned to German immigrant Levi Strauss, from whom he purchased some of his fabric. On May 20, 1873, Strauss and Davis received a United States patent for using copper rivets to strengthen the pockets of denim work pants. Levi Strauss & Co. began manufacturing the famous Levi's brand of jeans using fabric from the Amoskeag Manufacturing Company in Manchester, New Hampshire. Quite a riveting invention!

# THE ZIPPER (1891)

Though he was awarded over 30 patents during his career, the invention Whitcomb L. Judson is most known for is the zipper. It was called a "clasp-locker" in his day (it wasn't called a "zipper" until after his death). Judson's creation was a complicated hook-and-eye fastener with a guide. It made fastening the popular high-button boots of his day so much easier. Now they could be fastened in a "zip!"

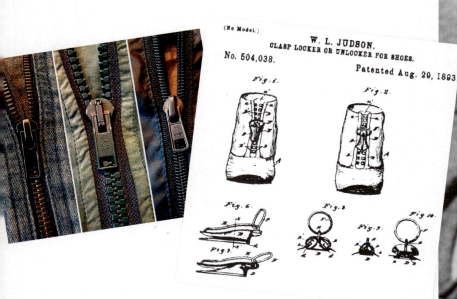

# SPANDEX (1959)

In 1959, chemist Joseph Shivers created a new synthetic fiber named Spandex (or elastane) while working at DuPont's Benger Laboratory in Waynesboro, Virginia. Spandex was stronger and more durable than rubber. Now Americans could wear clothing that would stretch and flex with their active lifestyles!

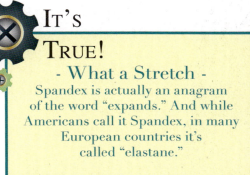

**IT'S TRUE!**
- What a Stretch -
Spandex is actually an anagram of the word "expands." And while Americans call it Spandex, in many European countries it's called "elastane."

# DIGITAL VISIONARIES

As America entered the computer age, innovative minds led the way. What was once science-fiction became shiny, new realities that made the United States one of the most technologically advanced countries in the world.

## CHESTER CARLSON – XEROGRAPHY (1942)

An engineer for Bell Telephone Labs, Chester Carlson wanted to be a lawyer. He studied law at night at the New York Law Library, copying down information in long-hand from the law books. His hands got tired and he wished there was a better way of duplicating the pages he needed to reference.

Hoping to find a solution to the problem, Carlson visited the science & technology section of the library. There, he found an article written by a Hungarian physicist describing how to electrically charge a rotating cylinder so an image could be transferred and printed. And after several years filled with smelly and fiery experiments, Carlson finally succeeded in photographically copying an original document. He called the process "xerography"—formed by combining the Greek words *xeros* (dry) and *graphein* (writing).

**How it works**
1. A drum is charged statically.
2. A lamp shines on the original document. Light parts of the original document reflect the light, dark parts don't.
3. The static charge on the drum is canceled by the reflected light.
4. The static charged parts attract toner, which sticks to the drum.
5. The paper is given a static charge.
6. The paper then goes past the drum. The toner sticks to the paper now.
7. Hot rollers melt the toner onto the paper where the copy is created.

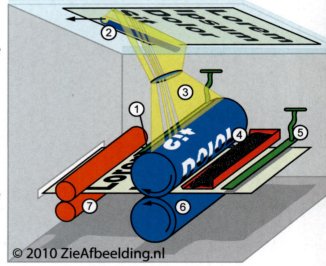

© 2010 ZieAfbeelding.nl

## JACK KILBY – INTEGRATED CIRCUIT (1958)

In mid-1958, Jack Kilby was a newly employed engineer at Texas Instruments. Because he was new, he had no vacation time, so he spent his first summer working to solve a company problem in circuit design called the "tyranny of numbers." He concluded that manufacturing the circuit components in a single piece of semiconductor material could provide a solution. Thus the integrated circuit or "chip" was born (though Robert Noyce is also credited as a co-inventor for independently creating a similar circuit a few months later). Not a bad way to spend your summer!

# Steve Jobs – Apple Computer

Though he dropped out of college after only one semester, Jobs and Steve Wozniak came up with the Apple Macintosh home computer (now called a "Mac"). The key turning point for the company came when Xerox's PARC gave them access to the technology in their labs for three days. The price? Xerox wanted the right to buy one million dollars of company stock. It turned out to be a great deal! In those three days, they saw the technology behind the computer mouse and the graphic user interface (GUI) we use on most computers today. Armed with this cutting-edge technology, Jobs and Wozniak came up with the Apple Macintosh home computer.

Jobs left Apple for a while after a dispute. During that time, he created Next computer (1985) as well as Pixar Animation Studios (1986). Eventually, he returned to Apple where he left a legacy of hi-tech products such as the iPod, the iPhone, and the iPad before his death in 2011.

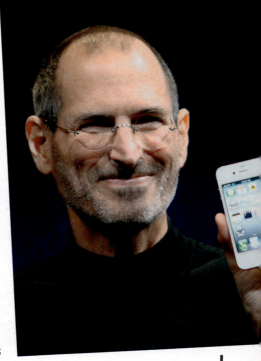

# Bill Gates – Microsoft

From the age of 13, Bill Gates was fascinated by computers. Soon, he learned to program them better than most adults. He was amazed at how a computer would execute software code perfectly. He wanted more time on the computer used by his school, so he exploited bugs in the system. But he and his future business partner, Paul Allen, got caught and were banned from the machine for breaking the rules. Ironically, at the end of the ban, Gates was invited back to find other bugs in the system. Gates was hooked!

Though he went on to attend Harvard University, he dropped out in 1976 to form a new computer software company with his friend, Allen. They called their new company Microsoft. Together, they went on to create the wildly successful Windows operating system, and their company, Microsoft, continues innovating to this day.

# Pierre Omidyar – eBay

Started in September 1995, eBay began in 28-year-old software developer Pierre Omidyar's living room in San Jose, California. Omidyar started his site (originally called AuctionWeb) to answer a question: what effect would equal access to information have on the marketplace? His first item, a broken laser pointer, sold for around $15. From there, the site just grew and grew. Soon he named the site "eBay.com," short for Echo Bay Technology Group, Omidyar's consulting firm. Before long, even "Weird Al" Yankovic was singing about all the things he bought on eBay!

# PLAYTIME!

Americans not only love to invent cool gadgets to make work easier, they also love to create new ways to have fun and put a smile on someone's face!

## Ferris Wheel (1891)

Though there were versions of a wheel with chairs prior to 1893 (William Somers made a 50-foot wheel the year before), bridge-builder George Ferris was the man behind the classic "Ferris" wheel. The largest attraction at the World's Columbian Exposition, Ferris' wheel was 264 feet. (80.4 meters) high and could carry over 2,000 people in 36 cars. Though today's wheels are typically smaller, the Ferris Wheel is still a crowd favorite at carnivals, state fairs, and amusement parks all over the nation.

## Skee-Ball (1909)

Invented by J. Dickinson Este in Philadelphia, Pennsylvania, in 1909, Skee-Ball featured a lane similar to bowling, but on a much smaller scale. Instead of pins, the ball leapt up a ramp to scoring targets. Ever since that day, Americans have been letting the good times roll!

### Famous Firsts

**- The Sweet "Wiff" of Success -**

Inventor David N. Mullany wanted a way for his son to play baseball without all the broken windows and pitching elbows. So he came up with a plastic bat and created a special plastic ball with holes in it. When the neighborhood boys would strike out, they'd call it a "wiff," and the name stuck – Wiffle Ball (1953).

## Mobile Popcorn Machine (1893)

What's a good time without popcorn? Though popcorn has been around for a long time, Charles Cretors was the first one to pop it in an automated machine. He would pop it right before your eyes with the savory smells hypnotizing every passerby. It certainly was a hit at the Columbian Expo in Chicago that year where there was always a line for his popcorn. You could say it became rather "pop"ular!

## Ruth Handler, Mattel & Barbie (1959)

Though her husband was a partner in the Mattel toy company, Ruth Handler could not get her husband to listen to her idea for a plastic doll with an adult body. Finally, on a trip to Europe, she found such a doll. She redesigned the toy and named it "Barbie," after her daughter Barbara. Barbie became an overnight sensation, so Handler added a boyfriend for Barbie called "Ken" (named after her son). It's been a Barbie world ever since.

## Teddy Bear (1902)

Candy shop owner Morris Michtom saw a political cartoon making light of a recent hunting trip with President Theodore Roosevelt. The President had refused to kill a captured bear, which inspired Michtom to create a little stuffed bear toy he called "Teddy's Bear" (with the President's permission, of course). They soon became such a craze that ladies carried them everywhere. Even children were photographed with them and when Roosevelt ran for re-election, he used one as a mascot!

## Electric Guitar (1931)

What could be more American than rock-and-roll? But long before Chuck Barry was singing about a country boy named Johnny B. Goode, George Beauchamp, Les Paul, and others were experimenting with attaching electric pickups to string instruments in the Roarin' '20s. Finally, in 1931, Beauchamp created the world's first working electric guitar, nicked-named the "Frying Pan" for its close resemblance to—you guessed it—a round frying pan. Together with Paul Barth and Adolph Rickenbacker, he formed the Ro-Pat-In Corporation (later named the Rickenbacker International Corporation). Together they went to work making electrified string instruments and amplifiers that would be used by the likes of The Beatles, The Who, The Rolling Stones, The Beach Boys, Jefferson Airplane, U2, Rush, The Pretenders, The Smiths, Muse, and the list rocks on!

### It's True!

- **High-Flying Cousin** -
Electric guitar pioneer Adolph Rickenbacker's distant cousin was none other than America's top WWI flying ace, Eddie Rickenbacker!

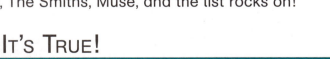

# Entertaining Ideas

Whether it's movies, television, theme parks, or video games, Americans have always found fun ways to educate and entertain.

## Walt Disney

If there ever was a home-grown American dreamer, it would be Walt Disney. Born in Chicago and raised in rural Missouri, Disney had an enthusiasm and vision that could not be contained—even by his brother and business partner, Roy. Disney was constantly on the cutting edge of entertainment. He led the way in creating the first feature-length animated film, *Snow White*, for which he received a special Academy Award. He even brought movies to life in 1955 when he introduced the world to the first fully-immersive "themed" amusement park he called "Disneyland." His company pioneered innovations such as Audio-Animatronics that the rest of the entertainment industry still attempts to mimic to this day.

## Nolan Bushnell

From his high school years working at Lagoon Amusement Park, Nolan Bushnell had a love for games and entertainment. Together with friend Ted Dabney, Nolan launched the video game company that would come to be known as "Atari." With the expertise of engineer Allan Alcorn (their first hire), they created one of the first video games, Pong. Other classic games by Atari included the Pong-related Breakout, Berzerk, Q*Bert, Pac-Man, Asteroids, Pitfall, Dig-Dug, Frogger, and Space Invaders. Wanting a place to feature his games, Bushnell later launched the Chuck E. Cheese's Pizza Time Theatre chain. He hoped it would give kids and their parents a place to eat pizza and play Atari video games. In an effort to add to the entertainment at his new restaurant chain, Bushnell even created an early computer animation company called "Kadabrascope." He eventually sold Kadabrascope to filmmaker George Lucas, and later it would be known as Pixar Animation Studios. Today, Bushnell continues his entertaining vision, making games to increase memory and concentration called Anti-Aging Games!

## TED TURNER

Competing in sailing competitions from the age of 12 (later successfully defending America's Cup in 1977), Ted Turner grew up in the media business. So when his father died while he was in college, Turner left school and took over his father's billboard advertising business at age 24. Gradually, he turned it into a media empire, creating the cable TV powerhouse TBS. Yet one of Turner's greatest contributions to entertainment had to be the creation of 24-hour Cable News Network, or CNN, in 1980. Never before had anyone devoted a channel to only news. Their exclusive coverage of events such as the *Challenger* space shuttle disaster and Operation Desert Storm only solidified Turner's position as an entertainment titan. His vision would help define the age of cable television.

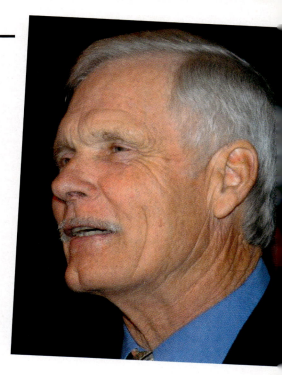

## JOAN GANZ COONEY

An aspiring actress and avid reader as a child, Joan Ganz Cooney always leaned toward a career in educational entertainment. After graduating with a degree in education, Cooney worked in television as a publicist. There she found out about a new educational television movement. Feeling it was her calling in life, Cooney launched into a crusade to establish a children's educational television company. She rallied several key people to her cause, and the Children's Television Workshop came into being in 1968. Their first show? *Sesame Street*, starring creative genius Jim Henson's muppets. Soon kids around the country would be singing, "Can you tell me how to get, how to get to Sesame Street?"

## FAMOUS FIRSTS

### - How 'Bout Them Apples? -

Nolan Bushnell once got a proposal by employees Steve Jobs and Steve Wozniak. They had created a personal computer and wanted to see if Bushnell would be interested in making and selling the new computer. Bushnell's answer? "No thanks. Atari is focusing on games." So Jobs and Wozniak packed up and formed their own company, Apple Computer.

# Young Innovators

Inventors and innovators come in all shapes, sizes, and ages. Many inventors got their start at a very early age, and you just may be one of them!

## Just a Child!

- Young Benjamin Franklin lived near the ocean in Boston, Massachusetts. He wanted to increase his swimming speed, so he invented swim fins! They were a bit stiff, though, since they were made of wood.

- 6-year-old Thomas Edison's experiments with fire were a bit more dangerous. He burned down his father's barn! He even got another kid to swallow gas-making effervescing powders to turn him into a human balloon. But all the kid got was a very horrible tummy ache!

## It's True!

### - The Exterminator -
Teenage Thomas Edison got tired of bugs invading his home. So he designed and perfected his first real invention—an electrical cockroach control system. He glued parallel strips of tinfoil to a wall and wired the strips to the poles of a powerful battery. It was a deadly shock for the unsuspecting insects!

## Teen Innovators

- 15-year-old Chester Greenwood was tired of coming home from ice-skating outdoors with frosted ears, so he had his grandmother sew tufts of fur between loops of wire. He later patented them as improved ear protectors in 1873. We know them today as earmuffs!

- Hiram Maxim created hundreds of inventions as an adult—everything from curling irons to single barrel machine guns. But when he was 14, he worked in a grist mill, and tired of the rodent pests, created an automatic mousetrap!

- One of 14-year-old Alexander Graham Bell's early inventions included a machine to remove husks from wheat in the flour mill run by his friend's father.

- Philo Farnsworth, inventor of the television, got his idea for optical scanning as a 14-year-old working on the family farm.

- In the summer of 1909, a 19-year-old dreamer by the name of Igor Sikorsky built one of the first helicopters. And it almost worked! After several years of work, Sikorsky perfected his design, and the dream finally flew into the wild, blue yonder!

## Do I Need a Patent?

Though many inventors love to share what they create, the U.S. government decided long ago that it was important to protect inventors by making laws called "patents." The first person to show the government a new idea or invention can apply for a patent. This means no one else can make something like it without the inventor's permission. But you have to apply for your patent within one year of making or selling your creation.

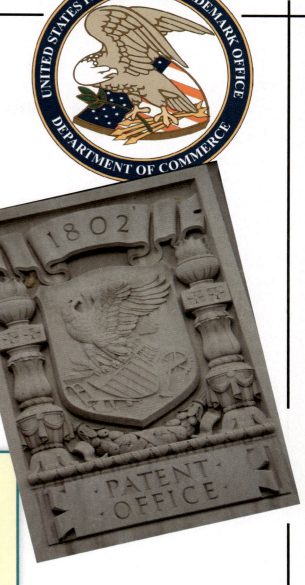

## Famous Firsts

### - The Epsicle -

In 1905, 11-year-old Frank Epperson accidently created ice pops. It happened when he left a drink outdoors on a cold night with a stir stick in the middle. Eighteen years later, in 1924, he decided to make ice pops and call them "Epsicles." But his kids made him change the name to "Popsicle," and it's been Popsicle ever since!

## The Innovator in You

Innovation begins with you and your imagination. Anything is possible if you are willing to work at it long enough. Don't be discouraged if your ideas don't work at first. Famous inventor Thomas Edison once said, "I have not failed. I've just found 10,000 ways that won't work!" So go out there, keep at it, and before long you may join the ranks of the great innovators and inventors of America!

# GLOSSARY

**Aerodynamic** – something designed to reduce the amount of air resistance or to make it easier to move through the air.

**Agricultural** – a word to describe anything to do with farms or growing crops.

**Astronomer** – a scientist who studies things in outer space such as stars and planets.

**Attendant** – someone who watches over an area of public use (like an arcade or a laundromat) to assist customers.

**Blacksmith** – someone who makes or repairs metal objects like horseshoes, weapons (such as swords), and tools.

**Carriage** – a wheeled platform that carries passengers or cargo.

**Commissioned** – to be paid money by someone to do something, like painting.

**Computer source language** – words or numbers used to give a computer commands.

**Crusade** – when someone tries very hard to do something and tries to get other people to join them.

**Delegate** – a person who is voted to attend a meeting of some kind and represent a whole group of people.

**Devices** – a tool or machine.

**Digital Age** – also known as the Computer Age or Information Age, the time we now live in where computers make it easy to find and share information.

**Encyclopedia** – a book or online resource with articles on different topics.

**Engineer** – someone who uses science to design things like new inventions (not the same as a train engineer who drives a locomotive).

**Epidemic** – when a disease spreads quickly; an outbreak.

**Expansion** – to grow outward in size.

**Exploited** – to use something so you can get what you want, often for personal gain and sometimes unfairly.

**Exposition** – a show or fair where artistic or scientific creations are displayed or demonstrated for others to see.

**Federal** – having to do with the government of an entire nation like the United States.

**Frequencies** – the particular wavelengths that radio and other similar waves travel on when they are broadcasted.

**Gauze** – thin, almost see-through material often layered to soak up liquids like blood or water.

**Graphic user interface (GUI)** – a computer program that allows someone to use pictures and icons to use a computer rather than typing in commands using letters, numbers, and/or symbols – like Windows on a PC.

**Gyroscopic** – having to do with a self-stabilizing or self-balancing device called a gyroscope.

**Hallmark** – a mark or action which someone or some company is known for; something they always do.

**Husks** – the rough outer part of a seed or grain like wheat or corn.

**Hydraulic** – a machine that is driven by fluid which causes pressure, in turn causing the machine to move.

**Industrial Revolution** – a period of time in the 1800s where there was a great focus on factories and new machines that made making things easier and faster.

**Intrusion** – to bother or interrupt someone.

**Marketplace** – a place, either real or on a computer, where people buy and sell goods or services.

**Merchant** – someone who buys and sells goods.

**Operating system** – the program that controls a computer.

**Pastime** – an activity that someone does in their spare time.

**Patron** – a customer; someone who visits a business to purchase goods or services.

**Physicist** – a scientist who specializes in physics, the study of matter, energy, force, and motion and how they relate to each other.

**Plasma** – a clear, yellowish liquid that blood cells travel in.

**Profitable enterprise** – a business or activity that makes money.

**Prohibition** – the period of time between 1919-1933 when making, selling, or transporting alcohol was made illegal by the 18th Amendment to the U.S. Constitution.

**Reaper** – a machine that cuts down fields of grain for harvest, such as wheat or barley.

**Refined** – to have made something better than it was originally.

**Refrigeration** – machines that make things cold.

**Revolver** – a gun that has several chambers to hold bullets and rotates when fired.

**Stone Age** – the earliest time period in human history, when men lived in caves.

**Terrain** – different types of ground such as rocky, or sandy, or dry, or wet, etc.

**Textile** – the name for cloth of all kinds, such as wool or cotton.

**Ton** – 2,000 lbs. (907 kg)

**Transcontinental** – across a continent, like North America or Africa.

**Vaccine** – a substance often containing a weak virus injected into the body to help it develop a defense against the virus or disease.

**Vulcanizing** – the process of treating raw rubber tree sap to strengthen it so it will not melt or break down at high temperatures.

# INDEX

Alcorn, Allan 40
Allen, Paul 37
Anti-Aging Games 40
Apple Computer 37, 41
Armstrong, Edwin Howard 20
Atari 40
Barth, Paul 39
Bath, Patricia 15
Beauchamp, George 39
Bell, Alexander Graham 16, 20, 42
Birdseye, Clarence 26
Bonaparte, Napoleon 12
Brady, Matthew 13
Burton Snowboards 33
Bushnell, Nolan 40, 41
Camp, Walter 32
Carlson, Chester 36
Carpenter, Jake Burton 33
Carrier, Willis 28
Cartwright, Alexander 32
Carver, George Washington 17
Children's Television Workshop 41
Chuck E. Cheese 40
Clermont, The 12
Clipper flying boat 19
CNN 41
Colt, Samuel 13
Cooney, Joan Ganz 41
Cooper, Martin 21
Cretors, Charles 38
Crum, George 27
Dabney, Ted 40
Dahl, Gary 7
Davis, Jacob 34
Dickson, Earle 24
Diemer, Walter 27
Disney, Roy 40
Disney, Walt 40
Drew, Charles 25
Eastern First Peoples 8
Eastman, George 21
eBay 37
Edison, Thomas 16, 21, 22, 23, 42, 43
Este, J. Dickenson 38
Evans, Oliver 11
Farnsworth, Philo 21, 42
Ferris, George 38
Fitch, John 18
Ford, Henry 23
France, Bill 33
Franklin, Benjamin 10, 11, 12, 42
Fry, Arthur 7
Fulton, Robert 12, 13, 18
Gates, Bill 37
Gildersleeve, Arthur 7
Goddard, Robert 30

Goodyear, Charles 18
Gray, Elisha 20
Greene, Catherine 14
Greene, Nathanael 14
Greenwood, Chester 42
Gregory, Captain Hanson 27
Halstead, Alfred 32
Handler, Ruth 39
Hardart, Frank 27
Henry, William 12
Henson, Jim 41
Hopper, Admiral Grace 15
Horn, Joseph 27
Hubble Space Telescope 31
In 'N Out 27
Inuit 8, 26
Jefferson, Thomas 11
Jobs, Steve 37, 41
Judah, Theodore 12
Judson, Whitcomb L. 35
Kamen, Dean 29
Kies, Mary 14
Kilby, Jack 36
Knight, Margaret 14
Kodak 21
Kroc, Ray 27
Kwolek, Stephanie 14
Lafayette, Marquis de 13
Lucas, George 40
Marconi, Guglielmo 23
Maxim, Hiram 42
McCormick, Cyrus 22
McCoy, Elijah 17
McDonald Brothers 27
Michtom, Morris 39
Microsoft 37
Morgan, Garrett 17
Morgan, William 32
Morrison, William 27
Morse, Samuel 13
Mullany, David N. 38
Naismith, James 32
NASA 31
NASCAR 33
*Nautilus* 12, 31
Noyce, Robert 36
Olds, Eli 23
Omidyar, Pierre 37
*Orukter Amphibolos* 11
Otis, Elisha 28
Pacific Railroad Act 13
Pan American Airways 19
PARC 37
Paul, Les 39
*Perseverance* 18
Pixar Animation Studios 37, 40

Poppen, Sherman 33
Prohibition 33
Raytheon 29
Rickenbacker, Adolph 39
Rickenbacker, Eddie 39
Rockefeller, John D. 16
Roosevelt, Theodore 38
Salk, Jonas 24
Samuelson, Ralph 33
Saturn V rocket 30
Scott, Edward & Clarence 29
Sesame Street 41
Shivers, Joseph 35
Sikorsky, Igor 42
Silver, Spencer 6
Singer, Isaac 34
Snowshoes
    Alaskan 9
    Bear Paw 9
    Michigan 9
    Ojibwa 9
Snurfer 33
Somers, William 38
Spencer, Percy 29
Spitzer, Lyman 31
Strauss, Levi 34
Teetor, Ralph 19
Tesla, Nikola 23
Thimonnier, Barthélemy 34
Totino, Rose 15
Transplants
    Bone marrow 25
    Lung 25
Trippe, Juan 19
Turner, Ted 41
Voigt, Henry 18
Wakefield, Ruth 27
Walker, Madam C.J. 16
Washington, George 11
Webster, Noah 13
Wharton, John C. 27
Whitney, Eli 10, 13
Woods, Granville T. 16
Wozniak, Steve 37, 41
Wright, Orville & Wilbur 19
Xerox 36, 37
Z Force 8
Zamboni, Frank J. 33

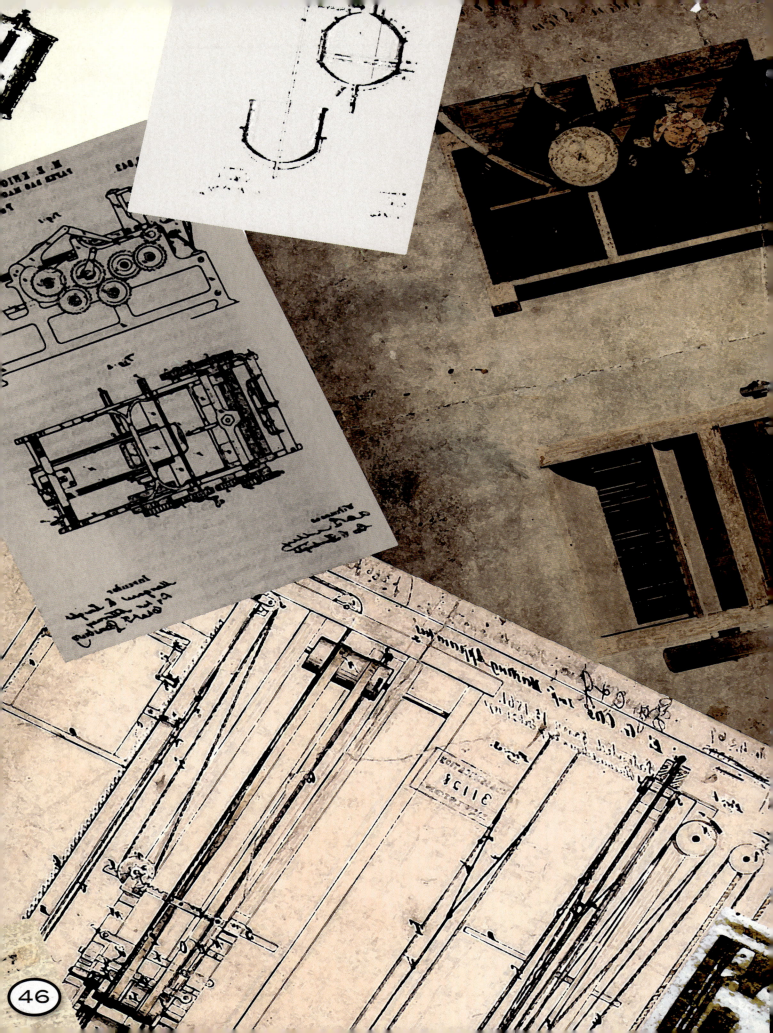